HIGHLY sensational women™

HOW TO BLOOM IN A HIGHLY CHARGED WORLD

Strategies for Success

LYNELL RAE

HIGHLY SENSATIONAL WOMEN™

First Printing, 2014

ISBN:9781502352910

highlysensationalwomen.com

DISCLAIMER: This book is not intended as a substitute for medical advice. The resources made available in this book are provided for informational purposes only, and should not be used to replace the specialized training and professional judgment of a health care or mental health care professional.

❋ Do you need more downtime than others?

❋ Do you have an acute awareness of other people's feelings?

❋ Do you often feel overwhelmed?

❋ Do you need more sleep than most people?

❋ Has your natural, kind openness been mistaken as weakness?

❋ Have you often heard, "You're *so* sensitive!"?

❋ Do you have a strong intuition?

❋ Have you been told that you are too intense?

YOU MAY BE A
HIGHLY SENSATIONAL WOMAN

Embrace this gift and learn to bloom in your natural environment. this book will provide you the tools, methods, and strategies to reveal the highly sensational woman within and help you to thrive in this super-sized, super-charged world.

You ARE sensational!

contents

ABOUT THE AUTHOR

Lynell Rae is a professional speaker and Certified Empowerment Coach. She enjoys writing, reading, scrapbooking, and spending time with her family. Lynell is a mom of four grown children and a grandma to thirteen grandchildren. She is engaged to be married. In the year ahead, she looks forward to reading many books, writing, and an 11-night Caribbean cruise (for her honeymoon).

ACKNOWLEDGEMENTS

No one walks alone on the journey of life. How does one start to thank those that walked beside you and helped you along the way? Perhaps this book will be a "thank you" to all those who have helped make my life what is today.

First, I would like to acknowledge Elaine Aron, whose inspiring book, *The Highly Sensitive Person*, changed my life. In her words, I saw myself and finally understood that, while I'm different, I am not alone. Thank you, Elaine, for your research and work with the twenty percent of us who are highly sensitive.

Much of what I have learned over the years has come as the result of being a mother to four wonderful children. Each of you, in your own ways inspired me. I also have to thank my thirteen grandchildren. You have taught me much about myself and the blessings in life.

Thank you to Patrick for your belief in me and in this book. You encouraged me and pushed me—without you, I do not know when I might have completed my writing. Special thanks also to all my cheerleaders for your helpful and invaluable assistance, support and guidance. I wish to express my love and gratitude to my beloved family, for your understanding & endless love through the years.

Last, but not least, I also need to thank a wonderful man who changed me completely—Richard, my fiancé. Your love has shown me my inherent worth and inspired me to be the best I can be.

WHO IS THE "HIGHLY SENSATIONAL WOMAN"?

❋ She is an intelligent, intuitive and imaginative woman.

❋ The HSW has great awareness of the subtleties in the environment and experiences things intensely; often feeling like an emotional sponge, overwhelmed by the world.

❋ She has a high level of compassion and is creative by nature.

❋ She has been referred to as "too sensitive", "intense", "touchy" or "high strung."

❋ The HSW has insatiable curiosity.

❋ She is most often right-brained and less linear than non-HSWs.

❋ The HSW has an inherent heightened sensitivity to all types of stimuli.

❋ Many HSW have felt flawed since they were very young, resulting in low self-esteem.

❋ The HSW may be an "empath;" highly sensitive to the energy of others.

❋ She may be more sensitive to pain.

❋ The Highly Sensational Woman may have a deep, rich, inner life and may be very spiritual.

{ "You absorb sensation the way a paintbrush grasps each color it touches on a palette. The ethereal beauty of a dandelion, the shift of a season, the climax of a song, or the scent of a certain fragrance can sometimes move you to tears"

Victoria Erickson }

One in five people are born with heightened sensitivity, according to author Elaine N. Aron. "Sensitivity is an inherited trait." It is found in equal numbers of men and women. The term "highly sensitive person" (HSP) was coined by Dr. Elaine N. Aron in 1996, and the name has gained popularity because it presents the trait in a positive way. Approximately 70% of Highly Sensitive People are introverts and 30% are extraverts. Dr. Aron has identified 27 characteristics of the HSP. If you suspect that you are highly sensitive, I would invite you to visit her website and take the self-test. (Aron, 1996) I have also included resources at the end of this book that you will find helpful.

"Every person is born with a particular temperament, a personality set point based on his or her genes," says psychologist Anett Gyurak, Ph.D., (Subramanian, 2012) who studies anxiety and emotion regulation at Stanford University. One gene in particular has been strongly linked to sensitivity. "The trait wouldn't survive in the gene pool unless it had benefits. Sensitive people are more careful, more alert to danger," says Gyurak.

In recent years, researchers have identified the Highly Sensitive Person (HSP) as a type of person who is emotionally and biologically more sensitive to all kinds of stimuli. The HSP has an ultra-sensitive nervous system; an innate heightened sensitivity to stimulation—sensory, social, or informational. Studies have shown that HSP's have more activity and blood flow in the right hemisphere of the brain, indicating that they are internally focused rather than outwardly oriented. Being Highly Sensitive is as physiological as hair texture or handedness. The Highly Sensitive Person's brain refines information into much more detail than other brains. (O'Rourke, 2012)

{
"I was the shyest human ever invented, but I had a lion inside me that wouldn't shut up."

Ingrid Bergman
}

In the HSP Intro Handbook (O'Rourke, 2012) being Highly Sensitive is likened to being left-handed:

- ✳ Both are a result of the makeup of the brain

- ✳ Both occur in a minority of the population

- ✳ Both suffer stigmas due to their differences

- ✳ Both have beneficial traits that come as a direct result from these differences

INTRODUCTION

{
"Continually swimming in an endless sea of sensation can at times be exhausting, regardless if it's beautifully terrible or terribly beautiful, and this is why your deep-rooted need for peace and self-care is essential to support your superb sensitivity"

Victoria Erickson
}

Being highly sensitive can be challenging. It can also be very rewarding. I am a Highly Sensational Woman (HSW), sensitive to many physical and emotional stimuli. My highly sensitive nature can create certain challenges in my day-to-day living. I can feel overwhelmed by crowds, noises, changes. Perfumes and colognes are known to give me headaches. I don't like tight or scratchy clothes and will change into sweats or pajamas as soon as I get home at the end of the day. It takes a lot of energy for me to be social and I need to balance activity with downtime.

Being Highly Sensitive also has its gifts—I am perceptive, compassionate, observant and passionate. I am open, receptive, and creative.

Wayne Dyer's message of our inherent worth has had a huge impact on my life. As a child I always had a sense that I was *forgetting* something. A "feeling" that there is something that I "know" but have forgotten. Something important, that no one else seems to remember either. Watching "The Shift" and reading Dr. Dyer's work, I found the answer. It was definitely an a-ha moment! *I had forgotten my worth.*

From the moment of conception we know our worth; then life happens and we "forget." The people in our lives have also forgotten their inherent worth. We learn that worth is measured by what we have, who we are, what we know. We constantly strive to feel "worthy."

Especially as a highly sensitive person, we are told and come to believe that there is something "wrong with us."

READING THE BOOK

The Highly Sensational Woman (HSW) needs a new way of understanding her sensitivity. By acknowledging her gifts and tapping into her strengths she can determine her optimum level of arousal and avoid feeling overwhelmed. Knowing how to soothe her senses when overstimulated is a critical part of coping effectively as a HSW. As a Highly Sensational Woman myself, I recognize that our needs may be somewhat different than the other eighty percent of the world.

The tips in this book are a collection from the research of other bodies of information and my own personal experience. It is my hope that these strategies will help you to understand your sensitivity, be aware of your feelings, and recover more quickly from over-arousal by learning how to respond.

Each chapter addresses a different topic and offers two steps to help you understand and cope with the unique challenges you face as a HSW.

The first step is to assess—recognize what is going on; identify your triggers. We have different stress-triggers, it's important to learn yours. Allow yourself to acknowledge feeling overwhelmed. In the book I refer to this step as *"checkpoints."*

The next step is to adjust—de-escalate feelings of being overwhelmed; when you're overwhelmed, your central nervous system shuts down the overloaded circuits. This step is referred to as *"action"* in the book.

Lastly, I invite you to respect your personal rhythm; honor your limits and your needs, and reframe your life. Your sensitivity is a gift; claim it and use it to create your best life.

CHAPTER 1

AWARENESS & SUPPORT

> "If the dimension of presence or awareness is missing, then you are lost in the reaction. Then you become the reaction and you don't know who you are."
>
> Eckhart Tolle

Understanding how you react energetically in the world is critical. Knowledge is power; know your limits; become aware of the internal signals that let you know you are reaching maximum capacity.

Knowing yourself and understanding why you're reacting the way you do can help you to stop comparing yourself to others and assuming that you don't measure up.

Checkpoint

Natural light is so important to my well-being. I am grateful for an office with a window. One morning as I worked at my desk, I noticed that I was feeling overwhelmed, agitated. As I checked in with myself, I realized that the activity outside was the culprit. They were paving the front parking lot; it was loud and busy. I immediately closed the blinds and almost as quickly found my nerves soothed.

When do you notice your feelings are overwhelmed? Are there specific places or events? What are some of your triggers?

Awareness

- ❋ Read about being highly sensitive; check your perspectives—see appendix.

- ❋ Checkpoints—tune in to yourself on a regular basis; observe how you react in different settings; identify your triggers.

- ❋ Assess and adjust (oxygen mask thinking); we only have a limited amount of energy. Just as they instruct when flying, it is critical that we secure our own oxygen mask before assisting others; Take care of yourself first so you can better "be" in this world.

- ❋ Value your gifts (insight, creativity, empathy).

Action

Be aware of your surroundings; recognize you feel anxious or overwhelmed as they first surface. Identify your triggers; avoid those trigger points when possible; take action to reduce the overload.

Complete the following:
I will begin to increase my awareness of my triggers by...

_____

_____

_____

_____

I feel overwhelmed/anxious when

_____

_____

SUPPORT

A strong support network can be critical in helping you to learn how to navigate life as a highly sensitive woman and reveal your greatness. It is invaluable to have people in our lives that genuinely care about us and accept us as we are.

This support network doesn't necessarily need to be professional or support groups. It could be coffee with a friend, a phone call to your sister, networking with other highly sensitive women on social media. These are all ways to develop and nurture lasting relationships.

BENEFITS OF A SOCIAL SUPPORT NETWORK

Numerous studies have demonstrated that having a network of supportive relationships contributes to psychological well-being. When you have a social support network, you develop a sense of belonging and increased sense of self-worth.

CHECKPOINT

Do you have a strong support network? In what environment do you feel a sense of belonging?

SUPPORT

- ✤ Network—connect with other sensitive people and with successful, not-so-sensitive people. Highly sensitive people can learn a lot from others.

- ✤ Surround yourself with supportive people who make you feel safe and secure—coach, mentor.

- ✤ Share "letter to friends and family of a highly sensitive person" (Axford n.d.). – See Appendix.

- ✤ Join support groups or form your own.

ACTION

Plant the seeds to cultivate deep, powerful and authentic relationships in which you can be yourself.

I will develop a stronger support network by doing the following:

_____

_____

_____

_____

"Maybe I'm too sensitive for this world."

Winona Ryder

CHAPTER 2:
PHYSICAL SENSITIVITY

"Your body is a temple, but only if you treat it as one."

Astrid Alauda

High sensitivity is a biological difference in the central nervous system. The Highly Sensational Woman (HSW) has an ultra-sensitive nervous system and her brain has far more filters than those who are not highly sensitive.

The physical body of HSW also carries traits of sensitivity and may have unique health concerns. Due to her sensitive nature, a HSW may experience more energetic blockages, greater chemical sensitivity, skin rashes and allergies. Research has shown that HSPs are thirty percent more likely to have allergies. It is vital for HSW to have a healthy, rested body to allow her to access her strengths.

Research by Michael Jawer (Placeholder2) found that highly sensitive people are unusually susceptible to an array of conditions such as migraines, irritable bowel syndrome, chronic fatigue syndrome, allergies and fibromyalgia. HSPs are unusually touchy to both emotional and tangible irritants—to mean-spirited comments as well as pollen or dander in the air.

CHECKPOINT

Emotional sensitivity can present itself physically. When I am stressed, I will experience increased flare-ups of rosacea and/or outbreaks of cold sores.
In what ways does your sensitivity present itself physically?

PHYSICAL AND BIOLOGICAL SENSITIVITY

❋ Drink a glass of water—drinking water supports nerve function; ensuring that your body's electrolyte levels remain high enough to allow your nerves to relay messages to and from the brain; drinking water boosts your energy and flushes out toxins; second to oxygen, water is vital to health.

❋ Walk near water – a river, lake, stream, fountains—the effects are calming and soothing.

❋ Take a bath—use daily baths/showers to wash off negative vibes and relax your muscles.

❋ Rest—when we're tired, we struggle to correct our systems.

❋ Sleep—adequate sleep helps to reset your emotional compass. the adult woman needs eight to ten hours in bed each day.

❋ Downtime—set aside two hours of downtime to meditate or putter. Your brain works overtime processing sensory input and needs time to recover.

❋ Play! Play helps to release endorphins, the "feel good" chemical. Endorphins minimize the perception of pain and reduce stress.

❋ Walk in nature—spend time regularly with animals, plants, near water and trees (or bring nature indoors); nature offers restorative, grounding energy.

❋ Get some sun/fresh air—fresh air is vital to health; it aids in cleansing your lungs, soothes your nerves and helps your body to get rid of accumulated toxins. Vitamin D increases serotonin, the mood neurotransmitter. Short exposure to sunlight increases the number of white blood cells and strengthens our immune system. Ten to 15 minutes of sunshine three times weekly is enough to produce the body's requirement of vitamin D.

❋ Diet modification—food sensitivities are common in highly sensitive people. Eat foods that are alkalinizing and more easily digested; avoid toxins in the foods you eat when possible.

❀ Maintain healthy diet—hunger arouses the intensity of any distress; keep water and healthy snacks available.

❀ Exercise—physical activity helps to keep your energy system operating efficiently; movement helps to get any environmental, emotional and energetic toxins out of your system. (Mills 2013) Specifically try workouts that incorporate your mind, body and spirit (Yoga, Tai Chi, Akido, Pilates, dancing, etc.).

❀ Drink herbal tea—tea has health benefits and drinking hot tea has a calming effect; Chamomile, a source of magnesium, is known as a soothing and relaxing herb.

❀ Recognize co-existing conditions (IBS, depression, anxiety, chronic fatigue, ADHD, etc.); there isn't much research to support the belief that there is a link between HSP and these other disorders; yet many highly sensitive people report having one or more of these conditions. Moreover, we recognize there is a cost to keeping our emotions inside and being socially acceptable. Turning feelings inward may contribute to other disorders.

❀ Adjust your posture—research shows that by adjusting your body posture, you can affect how you feel.

❀ Move your body—take frequent breaks; get up and take a short walk.

❀ Easy stretches—doing easy stretches (in your chair at work, on the train during your commute, etc.) helps to release stress and tension, boosts your mood and energy level, and increases circulation.

❀ Use sensitive skin care products.

❀ Use sunscreen.

To Aron, the evidence adds up to a distinctive personality type. The HSP's touchy nervous system leads to a touchy temperament. Like the princess sensing the pea below her tower of mattresses, HSPs perceive the slightest sensory or emotional provocation, then respond with a flurry of brain activity that begets an outsize reaction—rumination, tears, histrionics, on one hand, or unbridled enthusiasm on the other. Their personalities may run the gamut from moody to dramatic—all the product of their unique biology.

> "Health is defined as Inner Peace."
> Jerry Jampolsky,
> Author of *Principles for Attitudinal Healing*

ACTION

Can you link any physical conditions that might be induced by sensitivity?

_____

_____

_____

_____

What changes can you make?

_____

_____

_____

_____

{ Pure water is the world's first and foremost medicine.

Slovakian Proverb }

CHAPTER 3:
EMOTIONAL SENSITIVITY

> "At its worst, my sensitivity turns me into an emotional weather vane at the whim of my environment. But at its best, it's a gift, a fine-tuned finger on the pulse of every flutter of her surroundings."
>
> Jodi Fedor

The Highly Sensational Woman is sensitive to other people's moods and vulnerable to absorbing emotional junk from the environment. The nervous systems of highly sensational women are very fine tuned and she can become easily overwhelmed by emotional stimuli. She may be criticized for taking things too personally. The HSW may absorb energy from others, resulting in susceptibility to the attitudes, feelings, or conditions of others. Many Highly Sensational Women may be "empaths." She is a good friend. She is predisposed with a great potential and capacity for personal development and evolution because her spiritual energy field resonates at a high frequency.

Emotions are also a good source of data, which means that sensitivity can make people more insightful and open-minded, says David Caruso, Ph.D., coauthor of *The Emotionally Intelligent Manager*. (Subramanian, 2012)

CHECKPOINT

I find that my thoughts, feelings, emotions often swing wildly like a pendulum—from one side to another—within minutes. Like the changing wind, I go from one extreme thought to the contradictory, just as extreme, thought. Often I can observe myself—I recognize the thoughts as irrational—but I feel helpless to stop the craziness. And the discomfort and anxiety drive me to "doing something," acting on the feelings. It is important at those times for me to do nothing—to not *react* to those thoughts and emotions. Instead, I talk to a safe person, journal or meditate before acting on my thoughts. In other words, wait it out.

Do you find yourself *reactive* to emotions?

_____

_____

_____

_____

EMOTIONAL/SPIRITUAL

❋ Unplug—turn off your phone, shut down your computer, temporarily disconnect from the world.

❋ Small, manageable bites—we are often too quick to bite off more than we can chew; it is important to break it down to what feels manageable.

> Some time ago, a friend shared this riddle and it has stuck with me:

> Q: "What's the best way to eat an elephant?" A: "One bite at a time."

❋ Gardening—the sensory experience of gardening helps to relieve stress and improve overall wellbeing.

❋ Meditation helps to reduce stress; Judith Orloff prescribes quick, three-minute meditations during the day: Sit quietly, put your hand over your heart, deepen your breathing, and focus on something beautiful.

❀ Affirmations—affirmations can help to create a filter that blocks the negative energy of others and retrain your thought patterns.

❀ Reiki— Reiki and other releasing therapies help to purge negative energies.

❀ Keeping a journal will help to relieve mental stress and encourage reflection.

❀ Listen to your body—what is it telling you? Are you holding stress somewhere in your body? Are you hungry? Thirsty? Tense?

❀ Spend time with kids and animals; they are naturally open and sensitive.

❀ Get a massage—massage has been shown to reduce cortisol levels (stress hormones) and decrease the arousal level of the sympathetic nervous system; calming touch helps to reset our parasympathetic system.

❀ EFT (Emotional Freedom Technique)—HSW emotions are processed through pathways called meridians. EFT activates the meridian system and its endpoints to balance an individual's energy with a gentle tapping procedure; this helps the frozen energy to soften and move so that it can be discharged from the overwhelmed nervous system. "EFT reframes their beliefs in a gentle, positive way to honor their sensitivity." Rue Haas, M.A. (Rue Anne Hass n.d.)

❀ Embrace yourself—be gentle and forgiving.

❀ Participate in spiritual development.

{ "Healing may not be so much about getting better, as about letting go of everything that isn't you and becoming who you are." ~ Rachel Naomi Remen }

ACTION

Because we live in a fast paced world full of negative energy, good energy-management tools are imperative.

Which of these energy-management tools have you tried? Which might you want to introduce to your routine?

_____

_____

_____

_____

Sensitive to emotions: according to ancient Chinese medicine, emotions are processed through specific energetic pathways called meridians. A strong emotional impact can cause meridian blockage, which further leads to physiological problems. For an HSB (Highly Sensitive Body), emotions have a deeper impact to the body and easily cause blockage of the meridian. Thus HSB may experience more energetic blockages and imbalance in their lives.

"I'm an introvert... I love being by myself, love being outdoors, love taking a long walk with my dogs and looking at the trees, flowers, the sky."

Audrey Hepburn

CHAPTER 4:
NOISY

{ *"I think being different, being against the grain of society, is the greatest thing in the world."*

Elijah Wood }

The nervous systems of Highly Sensational Women (HSW) are very fine tuned and susceptible to stress. (Bartz, 2011) Clutter, whether it be environmental, digital or mental, decreases performance, increases stress and negatively impacts your ability to focus.

Sensory

HSW can be overwhelmed by sensory input such as crowds, bright lights, strong odors, loud noises, sudden movement, scratchy fabric, electronics, etc. These can be too noisy for the HSW, causing overstimulation and overwhelming feelings with which the HSW is unable to cope.

Checkpoint

When I was a child, my family would occasionally have dinner at a neighborhood tavern. I never wanted to go. For my brother and sister, this was a special treat and they would be excited. I sat in the backseat of the car, crying. I didn't understand why I felt the way I did; I only knew that it was horrible for me. I was chastised for crying. I was the "sensitive" one. What was wrong with me?

The tavern was dark, loud and smoke-filled. The burgers were greasy. At the bar, the men's actions were unexpected and clumsy. As a child, I had no control over the situation. It was excruciating for my sensitive nervous system.

What type of "noise" is most bothersome to you?

NOISY LIGHT

✳ Turn down the lights—adjust lighting (use heavy drapes, dimmers, etc.) and use natural light when possible.

✳ Wear sunglasses.

✳ Wear a sleep mask.

NOISY VISUALS

✳ Close your eyes—shut out stimulation.

✳ Surround yourself with pictures of nature, landscapes, calming colors (white, green or blue).

NOISY SOUND

✳ Turn down the volume.

✳ Turn off the radio in the car.

✳ Wear earplugs or headphones when it's not possible to control the volume.

NOISY THOUGHTS

✳ Clear your thoughts—quiet the noise in your mind, that incessant chatter.

✳ Add Epsom salt to your bath or soak your feet in Epsom salt water to clear away mental clutter; Epsom salts ease stress by replenishing the level of magnesium in our body. Toxins and heavy metals are flushed from our body with the help of sulfites in Epsom salt.

✳ Positive self-talk can be great for positive change in your thought process.

✳ Talk yourself calm—identify any fear or negative thoughts, speak them out loud and ask, "Is this about me?" Shine a light on those fears or negative thoughts and imagine them fading away.

✳ "Noisy" Odors

✳ Wear a mask.

✳ Burn candles or incense.

ACTION

Living in a highly-charged, fast-paced world we need to discover stress relief tools.

What can you do to turn off, turn down or turn on those areas that are troublesome?

_____

_____

_____

_____

"I get maxed-out more quickly than some, so it's my responsibility that I schedule little mini-breaks throughout the day, and have enough sleep. It's almost incumbent on me to make sure that I take care, in a very fierce way, in order to be able to continue to write and to be the person I want to be."

– Alanis Morissette

CHAPTER 5:
ENERGY

"I want all my senses engaged. Let me absorb the world's variety and uniqueness."

Maya Angelou

The Highly Sensational Woman is more sensitive to emotions and may worry about many things. She is often told she is too sensitive or she takes things too personally. The HSW often then tries to act like everyone else just to fit in. This can be very painful and cause her to lose touch with her true self.

Early on, I learned to be a chameleon – changing whom I was to fit in. My whole life I felt different. I believed that something was wrong with me. I tried to be what everyone else wanted me to be – to gain acceptance.

CHECKPOINT

Like a game, we're all trying to figure out who we are by watching others. We're hoping someone else has the missing pieces to our puzzle. It's only when we're whole that we can stop searching. A part of the process is building the frame and filling in the core sections, the same way you might build a jigsaw puzzle "Core" sections are the pieces that are our fundamental needs. My core sections include:

* It feels good for my home to be orderly, warm, textured.

* I need quiet, alone time; I need to balance activity/socializing with downtime.

* The rest is yet to be discovered.

What is core to being at your best energy level? What are your fundamental needs?

_____

_____

_____

_____

ENERGY—RECHARGE YOUR ENERGY LEVEL

❋ Fill your bucket—our energy level is easily depleted; it is critical that we find ways to fill our metaphorical bucket.

❋ Develop an attitude of gratitude—gratitude is a powerful stress relief tool.

❋ Speak your truth—release the negative and toxic thoughts.

❋ Massage your temples—massaging the temples helps relieves stress and relax other muscles as well.

❋ Center yourself—get grounded to detach from negative energy; be present in your body (refer to resources for grounding techniques).

❋ Sex—sex releases serotonin; it is important for a highly sensitive woman to have a partner who is caring and considerate.

❋ Wrap in blanket—a blanket made of silk or other natural materials can help soothe when you're feeling overwhelmed.

❋ Have comfort clothes—the HSW may be especially sensitive to textures.

❋ Create "white space" in your life; make room for the things that matter most by building in space "in the margins" of your life.

❋ Laughter is a great stress reliever.

- ❋ Take a few deep breaths to exhale negative energy. While you exhale, try to visualize all the negative energy coming out of your body with the air.

- ❋ Reframe—notice your thoughts, challenge those thoughts, replace the thoughts.

- ❋ Yoga—yoga reduces stress and increases energy; practiced regularly, it can also reinforce your relaxation response.

- ❋ Dance—dance helps trigger a rush of the mood-elevating hormone oxytocin.

- ❋ Expressing your creativity is a natural mood booster and has many benefits; it helps to quiet the mind and relieves stress.

- ❋ Painting—actually, any art form is beneficial, but there is something so therapeutic about holding a paintbrush. The brush strokes can alter your mind; research shows that some people with chronic pain reported that they feel no pain while painting.

- ❋ Visualization—use the power of your imagination to reduce anxiety, induce feelings of peace and calm, and bring on a general sense of well-being.

- ❋ Learn to focus—doing one thing at a time will help you to avoid being overwhelmed.

- ❋ Calm your mind; pause for reflection.

- ❋ Focus your breath—discover the power of your breath. Practice abdominal breathing by breathing slowly in through your nose and exhaling slowly and controlled through your mouth.

- ❋ Autogenic relaxation—deep relaxation technique (refer to resources). (Highly Sensitive People n.d.)

- ❋ Allow time to process the events of the day, limit evening activities after a busy day.

ACTION

What will aid in meeting your fundamental needs?

_____

_____

_____

_____

Their extreme responsiveness to all situations, Aron believes, makes HSPs prone to anxiety and depression in the face of a distressing situation. But it also makes life richer; sights, sounds, flavors, images of beauty are more vivid. It's as if HSPs alone see the world in high-def.

"The truly creative mind in any field is no more than this:
A human creature born abnormally, inhumanly sensitive.
To him... a touch is a blow,
a sound is a noise,
a misfortune is a tragedy,
a joy is an ecstasy,
a friend is a lover,
a lover is a god,
and failure is death.
Add to this cruelly delicate organism the overpowering necessity to create, create, create - - - so that without the creating of music or poetry or books or buildings or something of meaning, his very breath is cut off from him. He must create, must pour out creation. By some strange, unknown, inward urgency he is not really alive unless he is creating."
                                        Pearl S. Buck

CHAPTER 6:
ENVIRONMENTAL SENSITIVITY

> *"Treating myself like a precious object makes me strong."*
>
> Julia Cameron

The Highly Sensation Woman (HSW) absorbs energy from the environment and may experience difficulties in dealing with these stressors.

Michael Jawer's independent research points to wide-scale biological differences in Highly Sensitive People (HSP). As an investigator for the EPA, he looked into sick building syndrome and wondered why only a handful of people complain about indoor environmental conditions. The Highly Sensitive Body (HSB) is extremely vulnerable to toxins and stress. They can be easily overwhelmed by basic energetic frequencies and other harmful energies in their surroundings. The over-usage of electronics, computer and cell phone can create stress to the body.

Awareness of your sensitivities and caring for your Highly Sensitive Body will help to combat feeling overwhelmed and maintain or regain health.

CHECKPOINT

I am highly sensitive to perfumes, colognes, etc. This can be challenging when out in public. Have you ever been "stuck" in a small space with someone wearing strong perfume or cologne? It can be excruciating. I will experience severe headaches and nausea.

Unfortunately, there are times when I have no recourse except to wait it out; when feasible, I leave the area as quickly as possible. Other options might be to open a window or cover my nose with a tissue/hanky. It's important to 'detoxify' as soon as you are able—step outside, breathe in the fresh air or duck into the ladies room and splash water on your face and take some deep breaths.

The reticular activating system (the filter in the brain) should filter out excess sensory data, but for many highly sensitive women this filter has been compromised. HSW need to learn to develop filters in areas of their lives. What are some of your sensitivities to the environment?

ENVIRONMENTAL

* Use an Ionizer/air purifier to reduce toxins in air.

* Aromatherapy—spray essential oils on a scarf—when stressed, a sniff of the scarf will help to soothe your senses (see resources).

* Crystals are believed to help in boosting the immune system and protecting us from harmful electromagnetic pollution; some crystals are Mookaite, Amethyst, Jasper, Black Tourmaline.

* Burn sage—it's an ancient purifier.

* Use fragrance free detergents to reduce skin sensitivity and toxins.

* Smudge your home with sage to clear negative energy.

* Avoid toxins—detoxify your environment, use natural household products and personal hygiene products.

* Create personal space—it is critical that the HSW have a sacred, safe space for private time; a place you can retreat to when the world gets overwhelming. Make it simple but pleasing to all of your senses. (Shannon 2000)

* Turn off electronics—reduce the time you are sitting in front of a TV or computer screen.

* Reduce clutter—physical clutter, emotional clutter, the clutter of others; clutter not only takes up 'space' in your physical

environment, it also takes up space in your body, in your mind and in your emotions.

AT HOME

- ❊ Turn on music—pick tunes that calm you.

- ❊ Plan ahead—carve out downtime after an activity you know is a trigger.

- ❊ Create a daily routine—structure helps to reduce stress.

BOUNDARIES

- ❊ Develop boundaries for safety and comfort; often, highly sensitive woman struggle with maintaining healthy boundaries.

- ❊ Identify energy vampires—Energy vampires exude negative energy that drains you. On a subtle level these people suck you dry. Identify the energy vampires in your life and limit or eliminate contact. (Orloff 2011)

- ❊ Build an energy shield around yourself, either through visualization or by using essences (specifically Yarrow or Beech) or other holistic methods.

- ❊ Hit the "pause" button. Step back and allow yourself your emotional reaction. Reply, "Give me a minute to gather my thoughts," if you need time to process.

- ❊ Walk away—move outside the energy field.

- ❊ Disconnect physically or emotionally. If you can't walk away, disconnect emotionally; divert your attention to someone or something else in the room.

- ❊ Build internal strength—what makes you feel resilient?

- ❊ Give yourself time to integrate stimulation; in general, HSW need more time to process input.

- ❊ Learn to say "no"—this simple word makes a huge difference; offer no explanation—just say "no."

❁ "Sample;" try it out—our sensitive nature can be very unpredictable.

❁ Find your own optimal level of stimulation—we are all different and we all have different tolerance levels for stimulation.

❁ Balance social time and down time; balance work and play. If you need to spend time in the city, schedule time later in nature.

❁ Build in breaks between activities—allow enough time to avoid the frantic pace of running from one thing to another.

IN THE WORLD—SHOPPING

❁ Off-hours shopping—shop at times when stores are not as busy.

❁ On-line shopping—Internet shopping has become my preferred method of shopping

❁ Make lists, be prepared.

IN THE WORLD—TRAVEL

❁ When flying, if time allows, take the least crowded flight.

❁ Bring a soft blanket when traveling.

❁ Where a sleep mask to block out visual noise.

❁ Rest before travel.

❁ Have a protein snack ready when you need one—sensory over-arousal depletes blood sugar.

❁ Essential oils—sensitive people are vulnerable to taking on energy from others; flower essences may help ease feeling overwhelmed or anxious (see resources for remedies).

❁ Bring a portable fan—for white noise, take a fan, when possible, to use in your hotel room to block out external noise.

AT WORK

❁ Have a comfortable chair.

❋ When possible, create a pleasing environment—include personal items, plants, pictures of your family or pet.

ACTION

In what ways are you sensitive to the environment?

_____

_____

_____

Above all, HSPs are defined by their internal experience. "It's like feeling something with 50 fingers as opposed to 10," explains Judith Orloff, a psychiatrist and author of Emotional Freedom. "You have more receptors to perceive things."

What action can you take to filter out unnecessary or harmful input and minimize the discomfort in your environment?

_____

_____

_____

"I think I was born with a great awareness of my surroundings and an awareness of other people. I know when I really connect with somebody... Sometimes that awareness is good, and sometimes I wish I wasn't so sensitive.

Scarlett Johansson

CHAPTER 7:
POSITIVE TRAITS

"You have the ability to see colors and feel energy the way others hear jet planes. The world takes on a rich tapestry of immense gorgeousness at almost every turn, which then fuels your imagination and makes you spin with aliveness. And aliveness is a grand thing"

Victoria Erickson

I AM SENSATIONAL AND LOVING IT!

* The Highly Sensitive Woman is intuitive and tends to have deep spiritual experiences.

* She is a natural counselor, teacher, and healer because she has a compassionate, kind, and creative nature.

* Highly Sensational Women have a deep appreciation of arts and beauty.

* She experiences greater sense of love and joy than non-HSPs when not feeling overwhelmed.

* Highly Sensational Women are creative by nature.

* Her caring, sensitive nature tends to support well-being of all sentient life.

* Highly Sensitive Women tend to process information "more deeply" than others. They are predisposed to work well with

information technology because they are especially good at navigating through information. (Shannon, 2000)

❋ She has an insatiable curiosity.

❋ The Highly Sensational Women perceives subtleties that others may overlook because her 'skin' is not as hardened.

❋ She is highly conscientious and thorough; she makes a great employee.

❋ The Highly Sensational Woman has a rich, complex inner life and is highly imaginative.

> I was thinking that I might fly today. Just to disprove all the things you say... Please be careful with me, I'm sensitive, and I'd like to stay that way.
>
> — Jewel

ACTION

Identify your strengths as a Highly Sensitive Woman

_____

_____

_____

_____

_____

FAMOUS WOMEN THOUGHT TO BE **HSW:**

❀ *Actresses: Glen Close, Greta Garbo, Judy Garland, Audrey Hepburn, and Nicole Kidman*

❀ *Writer, Emily Dickenson*

❀ *Musicians: Janice Joplin, Alanis Morissette, Barbara Streisand, Jewel*

❀ *Artist, Georgia O'Keefe*

APPENDIX

Resources

Empath Remedies – Flower Essence Remedies for Easing Empathic Characteristics by Phylameana Lila Desy; About.com (Desy n.d.)

HSP Intro Handbook. http://www.plumturtle.com/PlumTurtleCoaching/Home_files/HSP_Intro _Handbook.pdf

The Highly Sensitive Hierarchy of Needs. www.sensitiveandthriving.com

Many actors, musicians, authors and other artists identify themselves as being shy, or consider themselves introverted or highly sensitive. See more at: http://highlysensitive.org/introverted-shy-highly-sensitive-arts/

Letter to Friends and Family of a Highly Sensitive Person. http://sensitiveandthriving.com/letter (Axford n.d.)

Are You Highly Sensitive? A self-test. www.hsperson.com/pages/test.htm

Coping With Stress In The Workplace www.Stressfocus.com

Academy of Creative Living. http://www.academyofcreativeliving.com/

3 Powerful Breathing Relaxation Techniques. http://www.stress-relief-tools.com/breathing-relaxation-techniques.html

Autogenic Relaxation Technique. http://www.stress-relief-tools.com/autogenic-relaxation.html

Aromatherapy Stress Relief - The Power of Essential Oils. http://www.stress-relief-tools.com/aromatherapy-stress.html

HSP Connections: Where the Highly Sensitive Person can find HSP-friendly web sites, groups, books, support, professionals, products, services and more! http://www.hspconnections.com/

Sense and Sensitivity.
http://www.psychologytoday.com/articles/201107/sense-and-sensitivity)

So Sensitive: Are You Tired of Sucking It Up? by Cheryl Richardson
http://www.cherylrichardson.com/newsletters/week-30-so-sensitive-are-you-tired-of-sucking-it-up/

Sensitive people may use their brains differently.
http://phys.org/news189932860.html

Highly Sensitive People: How To Thrive When The World Overwhelms You.
http://www.utne.com/mind-and-body/highly-sensitive-people-psychology-overwhelmed-by-the-world.aspx#axzz38WjbEe2x

Psychic Protection for HSPs.
http://ambergarnet.typepad.com/files/protection-for-sensitive-people-by-amber-garnet.pdf

Books

Aron, Elaine. 1996. *The Highly Sensitive Person: How to Thrive When the World Overwhelms You*.

Aron, Elaine. 1999. *The Highly Sensitive Person's Workbook*.

Aron, Elaine. 2000. *The Highly Sensitive Person in Love*.

Harwin, Cliff. *Making Sense of Your High Sensitivity*.

Mesich, Kyra. 2000. *The Sensitive Person's Survival Guide*.

Orloff, Judith. 2009. *Emotional Freedom*.

Zeff, Ted. 2004. *The Highly Sensitive Person's Survival Guide*.

REFERENCES

Aron, Dr. Elaine. *Are You Highly Sensitive?* A self-test. 1996.
www.hsperson.com/pages/test.htm

Axford, Ane. "Letter to Friends and Family." *Sensitive and Thriving*.
http://sensitiveandthriving.com/letter

Barnes, Sharon. "Seven Steps to Overcoming Overwhelm for Creative,
Highly Sensitive, Gifted People." *Academy of Creative Living*. April 2009.
http://www.academyofcreativeliving.com/uploads/Seven%20Steps%20to%
20Overcoming%20Overwhelm.pdf

Bartz, Andrea. "Sense and Sensitivity." *Psychology Today*. July 05, 2011.
http://www.psychologytoday.com/articles/201107/sense-and-sensitivity

Clark, Clint. "The Highly Sensitive Person or the HSP Sensory Nervous
System." *Insight Journal*, 2006: Wellness Concerns.

Desy, Phylameana. "Emath Remedies - Flower Essence Remedies for Easing
Empathic Characteristics." *About.com Guide Holistic Healing*.
http://healing.about.com/od/empathic/a/empath-essences.htm

Faey. "How To Protect Yourself From Negative Energy." *Emapth Solutions*.
http://empathsolutions.com/how-to-protect-yourself-from-negative-energy

Garnet, Amber. "Psychic protection for highly sensitive people." May 24,
2010. http://ambergarnet.typepad.com/london-
psychic/2010/05/protection-for-highly-sensitive-people-hsps.html

Harris, Erika. "Sensory Processing Sensitivity." *Lifeblazing*. 2011.
http://lifeblazing.com/sensory-processing-sensitivity/

"Highly Sensitive People." Stress Relief Tools. http://www.stress-relief-
tools.com/highly-sensitive-people.html

Kessler, Zoe. "Hypersensitivity: Are You a Highly Sensitive Person (HSP)?" *ADDitudeMag.com*, 2011. http://www.additudemag.com/adhd/article/8945.html

Mills, Edward. "14 Success Strategies for Highly Sensitive People." August 2013. http://edwardmills.com/2013/08/success-strategies-highly-sensitive-people/

Orloff, Dr. Judith. *Emotional Freedom: Liberate Yourself From Negative Emotions and Transform Your Life*. Three Rivers Press, 2011.

O'Rourke, Colleen. *HSP Intro Handbook*. Plum Turtle Coaching. Mar 03, 2012. http://www.plumturtle.com/PlumTurtleCoaching/Home_files/HSP_Intro _Handbook.pdf.

Rue Anne Hass, MA. *Artful EFT Work*. http://www.intuitivementoring.com/rues-work/artful-eft-work/.

Shannon, Maggie Oman. "Overwhelmed by the World?" *Utne Reader*. Nov-Dec 2000. www.utne.com

Subramanian, Sushma. "Are You Too Sensitive." *Women's Health Magazine*. June 13, 2012. http://www.womenshealthmag.com/life/being-sensitive.

Tartakovsky, M. "More Coping Tips for Highly Sensitive People." *Psych Central*. August 03, 2013. http://psychcentral.com/blog/archives/2012/06/21/more-coping-tips-for-highly-sensitive-people/

Underhill, Wendy. *The Low Down on Highly Sensitive People*. Nexus Pub. November - December 2006. http://www.nexuspub.com/journeys/journeys_highly_senstive_people.php

Zeff, Dr. Ted. *Tips For Coping*. http://drtedzeff.com/tips/coping/

Printed in Great Britain
by Amazon